Contents

A Special Day

Most people in Victorian times liked Sunday to be a special day. Victorians saw it as a day of rest, which God had given to them. Everyone had to be on their very best behaviour on Sundays.

A Day of Rest

Sunday was a day of rest, but you could not do whatever you wanted to do.

You could not:

- go to work (except some people, such as servants, had to work)

- play noisy games

- go shopping (but you could buy milk and bread)

Most Victorians had to go to church or chapel, once or even twice on Sundays. Some servants might have had the afternoon off after church, because Sunday was a day of rest.

▲ This is a Victorian calendar.

Sundays in VICTORIAN TIMES

Gill Munton

WAYLAND

Victorian Times

Christmas in Victorian Times

Clothes in Victorian Times

Schools in Victorian Times

Streets in Victorian Times

Sundays in Victorian Times

Transport in Victorian Times

How we Learn About the Victorians

Queen Victoria reigned from 1837 to 1901, a time when Britain went through enormous social and industrial changes. We can learn about Victorians in various ways. Many buildings built in Victorian times can still be seen today. We can also look at their documents, maps and artefacts – many of which can be found in museums. Photography, invented during Victoria's reign, gives us a good picture of life in Victorian Britain. In this book you will see what Victorian life was like through some of this historical evidence.

Editor: Carron Brown
Designer: Joyce Chester
Consultant: Norah Granger

First published in 1996 by Wayland Publishers Ltd, 61 Western Road, Hove, East Sussex BN3 1JD, England

© Copyright 1996 Wayland Publishers Ltd

British Library Cataloguing in Publication Data
Munton, Gill
  Sundays in Victorian Times
  1. Sunday – History – 19th century – Juvenile literature
  2. Great Britain – Social life and customs – 19th century – Juvenile literature
  390'. 09034
ISBN 0 7502 1830 4

Typeset by Joyce Chester
Printed and bound in Great Britain by B.P.C. Paulton Books

Cover picture: A mother reading a Sunday book to her children.

Picture acknowledgements
British Library Reproductions 15 (bottom), 26 (top); Mary Evans 22, 24, 26 (bottom); Billie Love Historical Collection cover, 5, 6, 10, 11, 12, 14, 18, 20, 21 (bottom), 25, 27; Mansell Collection 7, 17; National Trust Photographic Library 9; Peter Newark's Historical Pictures 8, 16, 19; Victoria and Albert Museum 23 (top); Wayland Picture Library 21 (top); Zefa 13 (bottom). The artwork on pages 7 and 9 is by Annabel Spenceley.

Thanks to Norfolk Museums service for supplying items from their museums on pages 4, 13 (top), 15 (top) and 23 (bottom).

All commissioned photography by GGS Photo Graphics.

A Family Day

Sunday was a family day. Most grown-ups were busy on the other days of the week, so their children did not see much of them.

Rich families had servants to look after the children on these days. These servants were called nurses.

On Sundays, though, children could spend the whole day with their parents. The children were, of course, on their best behaviour.

This photograph shows a rich family in 1888. ▼

Clothes

Do you like wearing your best clothes? Perhaps you choose them yourself. Most Victorian children were told what to wear, and they had to wear their best clothes on Sundays.

Sunday Best

A person's smartest clothes were called Sunday best. Boys often wore sailor suits, and girls wore long, frilly dresses. Both boys and girls wore hats. The clothes were not very comfortable, as you can see from the photograph.

It was easy to tear Sunday clothes because they had lots of frills and bows. They were often very pale in colour, so it was easy to get them dirty. Children sometimes had to change their clothes three times on Sundays! Many poor children did not have best clothes.

These Victorian children are wearing their Sunday clothes. ▼

Underwear

Victorian girls had to wear all these clothes under their dresses:

- a pair of cotton combinations
- a pair of woollen combinations
- a pair of stays
- a petticoat

Boys had to wear combinations too.

Washing Clothes

Most people washed their clothes every Monday. If a man only had one work suit, it was washed every Sunday so that it was ready to wear on Monday morning. If the man did not have any best clothes to wear on Sundays, he had to stay in bed while his work suit was being washed.

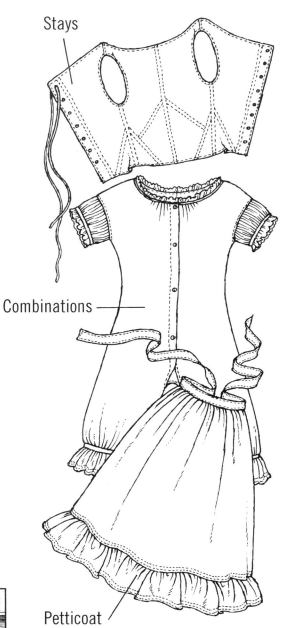

Stays

Combinations

Petticoat

◀ This picture shows a poor London family on a Sunday morning. The mother is doing some washing.

Food

In Victorian times, some families were very poor. They did not have enough to eat, and their food was very plain. If they could afford any treats, they had them on Sundays. Rich families often ate very big meals, especially on Sundays.

◄ This family is eating a simple breakfast of eggs and bread, and drinking coffee.

Breakfast

Poor families ate bread with jam or lard for breakfast, and drank tea. They saved extra food, such as eggs, for the father to eat on Sunday.

Rich families often ate huge breakfasts on Sundays. Here are some of the things they ate and drank (sometimes all in one meal):

- eggs
- kidneys
- bacon
- sausages
- chops
- ham
- tongue
- pies
- muffins
- toast
- tea
- coffee

Dinner

Most people ate their Sunday dinner at lunchtime, but rich families ate in the evening.

Sunday was the only day when some families could afford meat for dinner. They often had meat pudding. If they could afford a large piece of meat, they roasted it in an oven, or over a fire on a spit.

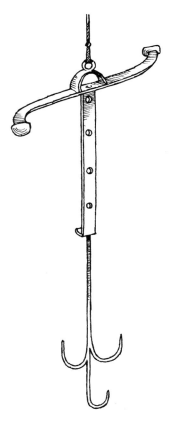

▲ This is a spit. It is used for cooking meat over a fire.

Cooking

This photo shows a kitchen range. If a family could afford a range, they could cook lots of food at the same time.

Some poor families had nowhere to cook food. They sometimes took their Sunday dinners to the local baker's shop, where the baker cooked them in his big oven.

This is a Sunday dinner menu from the 1880s. A builder and his family, who lived in Oxfordshire, served it to some relatives who visited them for the day. They had one servant to help with the cooking.

- Roast leg of lamb
- Two boiled chickens with slices of ham
- Jellies and cheesecakes

Tea

Tea was the last meal of the day for poor families. They ate bread and butter, or sometimes a special Sunday cake, and drank tea.

Rich families had afternoon tea, and ate dinner later in the evening.

Friends and relatives often invited each other for tea, especially in later Victorian times, when more people went out on Sundays.

These people are having Sunday tea in the garden. ▼

Servants

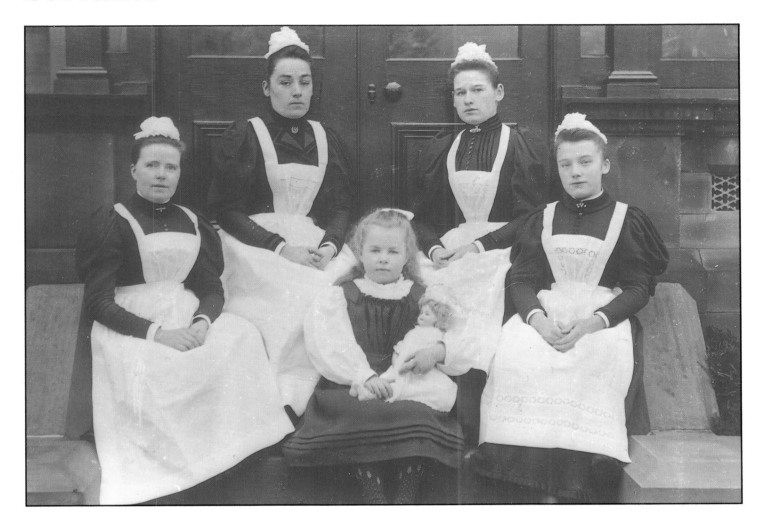

If they could afford it, Victorian people employed poorer people as servants, to help with the cooking and the housework. Some families had just one servant, while some had many more.

Some servants had Sunday afternoons off. This only happened after the main meal of the day if it had been served in the afternoon and not in the evening.

▲ This photograph was taken in 1898. It shows four servants sitting outside the house where they work. The little girl in the middle is the daughter of the family who own the house.

Going to Church

Many families went to church or chapel every Sunday. Children had to sit quietly until the long service was finished.

▼ This is a church on the Isle of Wight.

Different types of Church and Chapel

Most people in England and Wales belonged to the Church of England. In Scotland, most people belonged to the Presbyterian Church of Scotland. Other people were members of the Roman Catholic Church.

There were new chapels, too, and some people started going to them because they liked the lively new services. These people were called Methodists and Baptists.

Most people went to church in Victorian times. In villages, children who did not go to church on Sundays were sometimes punished at school on Mondays.

The Church of England

Most people in England and Wales had a local church, and rich families were allowed to buy or rent the best pews. They brought cushions to church to make the hard pews comfortable.

Poorer people had to stand at the back of the church, and they did not always feel very welcome. Some started going to the new chapels instead.

This photograph shows the inside of a church in the town of King's Lynn, in Norfolk. ▶

The Church of Scotland

In Scotland, the Presbyterian Church of Scotland had the most members. Other people belonged to the Episcopal Church.

As well as Roman Catholics, Baptists and Methodists, there were people who went to the new Free Church.

▲ This photograph shows a church in the Scottish Highlands.

◀ These children are singing a hymn in a church service.

The Services

In the Church of England and the Presbyterian Church, the services followed the same pattern every Sunday. Chapel services were different each week. Sometimes a visiting preacher came, to tell the story of how he started to believe in Jesus and lead a good life.

Sermons were an important part of the services in churches and chapels. The preachers tried to make people feel ashamed of the things they had done wrong, and grateful for God's gifts.

City Missions

The Church of England and the chapels wanted to tell poor people in the big cities about God, and to help them live better lives. They set up City Missions and invited people to special services and meetings.

This is a poster for a City Mission meeting. ▼

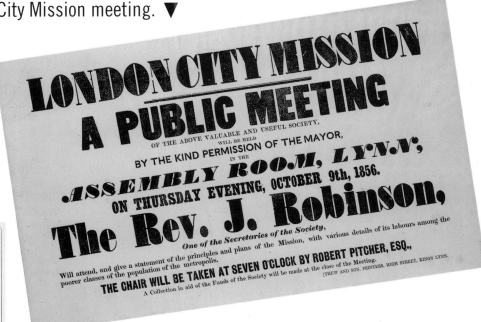

This is the first page of the catechism. ▼

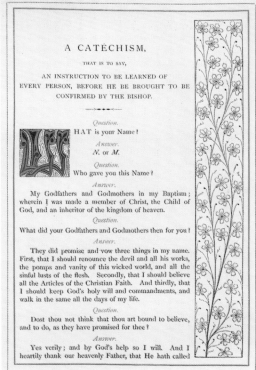

A CATECHISM,

THAT IS TO SAY,

AN INSTRUCTION TO BE LEARNED OF EVERY PERSON, BEFORE HE BE BROUGHT TO BE CONFIRMED BY THE BISHOP.

Question.

WHAT is your Name?

Answer.

N. or M.

Question.

Who gave you this Name?

Answer.

My Godfathers and Godmothers in my Baptism; wherein I was made a member of Christ, the Child of God, and an inheritor of the kingdom of heaven.

Question.

What did your Godfathers and Godmothers then for you?

Answer.

They did promise and vow three things in my name. First, that I should renounce the devil and all his works, the pomps and vanity of this wicked world, and all the sinful lusts of the flesh. Secondly, that I should believe all the Articles of the Christian Faith. And thirdly, that I should keep God's holy will and commandments, and walk in the same all the days of my life.

Question.

Dost thou not think that thou art bound to believe, and to do, as they have promised for thee?

Answer.

Yes verily; and by God's help so I will. And I heartily thank our heavenly Father, that He hath called

The Catechism

You can find the catechism in the Book of Common Prayer. It is a set of questions and answers which children had to learn by heart. This was to help them to understand what it meant to be a Christian.

Sunday School

Many children liked going to Sunday School. If a child went every week, he or she could win a prize, and there was the Sunday School treat to look forward to.

What Sunday School Was For

These children are walking to Sunday School. ▼

The churches and chapels set up Sunday Schools because they wanted to teach children about Jesus.

Day schools were expensive, and so many poor children could not go to them. Sunday School teachers often had to teach the children to read and write before they could teach them about the Bible. Almost all children went to Sunday School even if they did not go to school on other days.

Children could go to Sunday School in the morning, or in the afternoon after church.

Sunday School Teachers

In many church Sunday Schools, the teacher was the wife or daughter of the clergyman. Teachers in chapel Sunday Schools were sometimes chosen because they were good Christians, not because they were good teachers.

There were also assistant teachers, and the older children helped with the teaching as well. The children were taught in small groups. The only books were Bibles and copies of the catechism.

▲ This picture shows a Sunday School teacher with her class, in 1885.

Sunday School Prizes

Prizes were given to Sunday School pupils for good behaviour. The prizes were certificates and books. If children were naughty they were caned.

Every year there was an outing or treat for all the children.

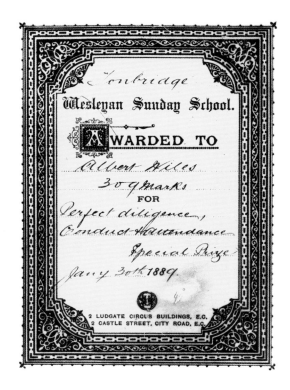

This is a Sunday School certificate, from 1889. ▶

Singing Hymns

Singing hymns made a change from studying the Bible. Some hymns, like this one, were written specially for children:

Do no sinful action,
Speak no angry word;
Ye belong to Jesus,
Children of the Lord.

This picture shows children singing a hymn in Sunday School, in 1896. ▶

Sunday Magazines

Several magazines were written specially for children. There were stories about poor children who did not know about Jesus, and stories about parents who could not look after their children because they drank too much alcohol.

In 1847, the Band of Hope was formed. Its members were against all alcoholic drinks.

This copy of *Our Own Magazine* was printed in 1894. ▼

Going Out

Victorian children did not have as many days out as children do now. The Sunday Schools organized most of their outings. The children looked forward to them and enjoyed them very much.

The Parade

Every year, each Sunday School held a parade on its 'birthday'. All the children marched along carrying banners, singing hymns and reading poems. After the parade they all had tea.

The Avenue Road Sunday School was formed in 1871. This is a photograph of their parade. ▼

The Sunday School Treat

In country areas, children travelled to the Sunday School treat by horse and cart. One Sunday School in Hampshire used a steam engine to pull the cart. The sparks from the engine made holes in the children's clothes!

Some Sunday Schools took children to the seaside or on a boat trip. There was always a large tea, and then games such as 'tag' or 'scrambling' for sweets and nuts.

▲ This is a Victorian steam engine.

For these children, the Sunday School treat was a trip on a canal boat. ▶

Things to Do

Sunday was a holy day. Children had to be quiet and serious, and most games and hobbies were not allowed. They had to find other ways of filling the long hours after church and Sunday School.

The Family on Sunday

On Sunday, most families sat together and read the Bible. The father also read his Sunday newspaper but the children were not allowed to disturb him. Later, just before the family went to bed, they said their prayers.

This picture shows a Victorian family at home on a Saturday evening. Before bedtime, they will put away the children's toys and the mother's sewing. ▶

Toys

On Sundays, children were only allowed to play with toys that taught them stories from the Bible.

Noah's Arks were popular, and so were jigsaws and brick puzzles showing scenes from the life of Jesus.

This photograph shows a wooden Noah's Ark, with Noah and his family, and all the animals in pairs. ▶

These bricks fit together to show scenes from the life of Jesus. ▶

The Afternoon Walk

Many families went for a walk on Sunday afternoons. The children had to be on their best behaviour, but it was better than staying at home with nothing to do. They could meet their friends, and show off their best Sunday clothes.

This picture shows a family walking in Hyde Park, in London. The boys are allowed to sail their boats. ▼

▲ These people are having a picnic tea of sandwiches and buns.

Having a Picnic

Sometimes families met their friends or relatives for a picnic. They usually walked, because people did not use trains or carriages on Sundays.

Visiting friends and relatives on Sundays became quite popular towards the end of Queen Victoria's reign. In Victorian times, most people lived quite close to their relatives. Sunday was the ideal day when they could all meet up and exchange news.

Books

Many popular books were about the Christian religion. The most famous one is *The Pilgrim's Progress* by John Bunyan. Children found this book difficult to read because it had been written 200 years earlier, for grown-ups.

Some books were written specially for children. Two of these books were *The Infant's Progress* and *The Fairchild Family* by Mrs Sherwood.

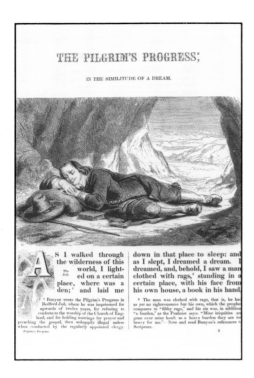

▲ This is the first page of *The Pilgrim's Progress*.

All these books were about people who tried to be good Christians.

Music

There were no radios or tapes in Victorian times, so people had to make their own music. Only religious music was allowed on Sundays.

This picture shows a Victorian family singing hymns around a piano. ▲

Saying Prayers

Victorian children had to say their prayers
every night before they went to bed.
Sometimes they said the Lord's Prayer,
and sometimes they said special children's
prayers such as this one:

Now I lay me down to
    sleep,
I pray the Lord my soul to
    keep;
And if I die before I wake,
I pray the Lord my soul to
    take.

This girl is saying her prayers
before she goes to bed. ▶

Timeline

BC	**AD 0**		**500**	
		43	**410**	
			'The Dark Ages'	
Celts		**Roman Britain**	**Anglo-Saxons**	**Vikings**

1800–1830

1803
The Sunday School Union is formed to help Sunday Schools in their work.

1818
The Fairchild Family, written by Mrs Sherwood, is published.

1819
Queen Victoria is born.

1830–1840

1831
The Lord's Day Observance Society is formed, to keep Sunday a special day of rest and worship.

1837
Victoria becomes queen.

1840–1850

1846
The young Prince of Wales is often seen wearing a sailor suit. This becomes a popular fashion for boys.

1847
The Band of Hope is formed, to stop people drinking alcohol.

1850–1860

1851
Queen Victoria buys Balmoral Castle in Scotland. Tartan becomes a popular pattern for clothes.

1000			1500					2000
1066			1485	1603	1714	1837	1901	
Middle Ages			Tudors	Stuarts	Georgians	Victorians	20th Century	
Normans								

1860–1870

1861
Dr Barnardo's East End Mission is formed in London, to help homeless boys.

1866
Alice's Adventures in Wonderland, written by Lewis Carroll, is published.

1870–1880

1871 The first Bank Holiday is enjoyed in Britain.

1880–1890

1886
Little Lord Fauntleroy is published. Velvet suits become a popular fashion for boys, because Little Lord Fauntleroy wore them.

1890–1920

1901
Queen Victoria dies.

Glossary

Banners Large flags that are held up by long poles at the sides.

Caned Hit with a long stick. This was a punishment used in Victorian times.

Carriages Horse-drawn vehicles.

Clergyman A man who holds church services and looks after the people who come to the church.

Combinations Underwear – vest and pants joined together.

Lard Fat from a pig, sometimes used for cooking.

Meat pudding Small pieces of meat rolled into a dumpling and boiled in a cloth.

Muffins Buns made with yeast.

Pews The long, wooden seats in a church.

Range A large cooker with one or more ovens which were heated by a fire inside.

Spit A piece of metal used for cooking meat over a fire.

Stays Padded vests, laced up at the front.

Tag A chasing game. One child chases after a group of other children to try to catch one of them. The child who is caught then becomes the chaser.

Books to Read

Non-fiction
Steel, A., *Victorian Children* (Wayland, 1992)

Triggs, T., *Victorian Britain* (Wayland, 1990)

Fiction
Barber, A., *The Mousehole Cat* (Walker Books, 1990)

Hill, S., *Beware, Beware* (Walker Books, 1993)

Hodgson Burnett, F., *The Secret Garden* (First published 1911; Gollancz, 1993)

Lively, P., *Fanny and the Monsters* (Mammoth Books, 1991)

Rogers, E. and P., *Our House* (Walker Books, 1992)

Places to Visit

The following museums have displays on Victorian times.

England
Avon: Blaise Castle House, Henby, Bristol, BS10 7QS. Tel: 01272 506789

Cheshire: Quarry Bank Mill, Styal, SK9 4LA. Tel: 01625 527468

County Durham: North of England Open Air Museum, Beamish, DH9 0RG. Tel: 01207 231811

Humberside: Wilberforce House, 25 High Street, Hull, HU1 3EP. Tel: 01482 593902

Lancashire: Museum of Childhood, Lancaster, LA1 1YS. Tel: 01524 32808

London: Victoria and Albert Museum, South Kensington, SW7 2RL. Tel: 0171 9388500
Museum of Childhood, Cambridge Heath Road, London, E2 9PA. Tel: 0181 9802415

Merseyside: Toy Museum, 42 Bridge Street Row, Chester, CH1 1RS. Tel: 01244 346297

Norfolk: Gressenhall Rural Life Museum, Dereham, NR20 4DR. Tel: 01362 860563

Shropshire: Iron Bridge Gorge Museum, Blists Hill Site, Telford, TS8 7AW. Tel: 01952 433522

Warwickshire: St John's House Museum, Warwick, CV34 4NF. Tel: 01926 412034

Yorkshire: Castle Museum, York, YO1 1RY. Tel: 01904 653611

Scotland
Angus: Angus Folk Museum, Glamis, Forfar, DD8 1RT. Tel: 01307 464123

Wales
Cardiff: Welsh Folk Museum, St Fagans, CF5 6XB. Tel: 01222 569441

Index